CUTTING EDGE MEDICINE

Fighting Infectious Diseases

Carol Ballard

FRANKLIN WATTS
LONDON • SYDNEY

First published in 2007 by
Franklin Watts
338 Euston Road
London NW1 3BH

Franklin Watts Australia
Hachette Children's Books
Level 17/207 Kent St, Sydney, NSW 2000

Produced by Arcturus Publishing Limited,
26/27 Bickels Yard, 151–153 Bermondsey Street, London SE1 3HA

Editor: Alex Woolf
Designer: Nick Phipps
Consultant: Dr Eleanor Clarke

Picture credits:
Science Photo Library: 5 (BSIP, Laurent/FILIN), 6 (Astrid and Hanns-Frieder Michler), 8, 10
(Sheila Terry), 13 (Volker Steger, Peter Arnold, Inc.), 14 (CNRI), 17 (D. Phillips), 19, 21
(NIBSC), 23 (Steve Gschmeissner), 25 (Andrew Syred), 27 (Sinclair Stammers), 28 (Juergen
Berger), 30 (Stem Jems), 33, 35 (John Walsh), 37 (Bob Gibbons), cover and 38 (Saturn
Stills), 41 (AJ Photo/Hop Americain), 43 (TH Photo-Werbung), 45 (Geoff Tompkinson), 47
(Geoff Tompkinson), 48 (James King-Holmes), 50 (AJ Photo), 53 (Dr Kari Lounatmaa), 54
(Philippepsaila), 57 (NASA), 59 (Pascal Goetgheluck).

Every attempt has been made to clear copyright. Should there be any inadvertent omission,
please apply to the publisher for rectification.

A CIP catalogue record for this book is available from the British Library

Dewey Decimal Classification Number: 616.9

ISBN: 978 0 7496 6968 3

Printed in Singapore

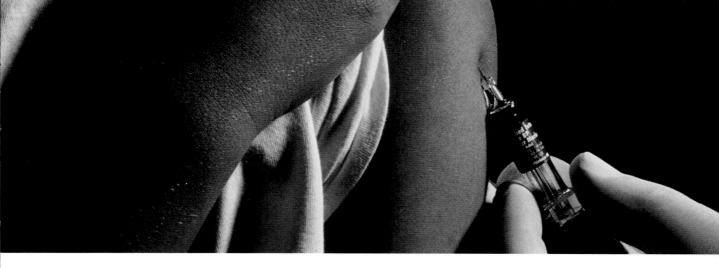

Contents

CHAPTER 1

What are Infectious Diseases?

An infectious disease is an illness that passes from one person to another. For example, if one person in a family has a bad cold, it often spreads to other family members. A common cold is therefore an infectious disease. Other examples include chickenpox, influenza (often called flu) and measles. Illnesses such as asthma, arthritis and heart disease do not spread from one person to another and so they are not infectious diseases.

Almost everybody in the world is affected by an infectious disease at some time during their life. Some infectious diseases are mild, some are serious and others are life-threatening. For example, a cold makes you uncomfortable for just a few days, but measles can make you feel very ill and may have long-term effects – and typhoid can rapidly kill large numbers of people.

CUTTING EDGE MOMENTS

The beginning of epidemiology

One of the first people to study the spread of infectious diseases was John Snow, who lived in London in the nineteenth century. Snow was appalled by the squalid living conditions of many people and was convinced that the lack of clean water contributed to the number of infections they suffered. In 1854 he studied the way an infection spread during a cholera outbreak in London. This allowed him to trace its source to a contaminated water pump. By removing the pump handle, he stopped any more contaminated water from being used, and this stopped the infection from spreading any further. Snow's method of studying outbreaks of infection gave rise to the science we now call epidemiology. Modern scientists who study the occurrence, frequency and spread of infectious diseases are called epidemiologists.

This woman has a cold, which is an infectious disease.

Killer diseases

Millions of people around the world die each year from infectious diseases. We know this because information about the health of the population in each country is collected by the World Health Organization (WHO). This information is then put together to give a global picture. Some of the information collected tells us the total number of people who die each year from different diseases. In 2002, the total world population was 6.2 billion, and a total of 57 million people died. Out of these, about a quarter of all deaths were due to infectious diseases. The biggest killers were pneumonia and HIV/AIDS. Next came diarrhoeal diseases such as cholera and typhoid, followed by tuberculosis (TB) and malaria. There are many possible causes of infectious disease. Cramped living conditions, poverty, lack of a sanitary water supply, poor nutrition, economic class, famine and drought all play a hand in diseases that rage out of control, especially in developing countries.

Infectious diseases and the human body

Understanding how the human body is organized can help us to understand infectious diseases, how they affect the body and how the body responds to them. The human body, like all other living things, is made up of millions of tiny units called cells. A cell is the smallest complete unit of a living organism. Cells that have a similar structure and function are grouped together to make tissues. Tissues are grouped together into organs, which are parts that carry out a single function.

Organs that carry out similar or connected functions are grouped together to make systems. For example, muscle cells are grouped together to make muscle tissue. Together, muscle tissues and nerve tissue make an organ, the heart. The heart, the blood vessels and

The food in this picture has not been stored properly and could cause an infection if it is eaten.

CUTTING EDGE SCIENCE

How do infectious diseases pass from person to person?
This table shows some of the ways by which an infectious disease can spread:

how infection is spread	example	diseases spread in this way
direct contact	a) touch b) mixing body fluids such as saliva and blood	impetigo – a skin infection HIV/AIDS
airborne	germs released into the air by coughs and sneezes	influenza, colds
food	inadequate storage or cooking	salmonella – a type of food poisoning
water	germs from poor sanitation and lack of clean water	cholera, typhoid
insects	insects can carry infection and pass it on to people by biting	malaria

the blood itself together make up the circulatory system, which maintains the circulation of blood around the body.

Just about every part of the body can suffer from an infection. Some infectious diseases affect a single organ or system while others may affect several organs. In some infections the effects are due simply to the infection itself. Some other infections produce toxins (poisonous chemicals) that can have serious effects. Other infections do little damage themselves, but the body's reaction to the infection causes serious effects.

Common or rare

Some infectious diseases, such as a cold or sore throat, are quite common. Many people suffer from them, sometimes several times a year. Other diseases, such as tetanus, are rare because there is an effective immunization program for them. Some infectious diseases occur all year round while others are more common in one season than another. For example, more people suffer from influenza in the winter than in the summer.

The infectious diseases that are common vary from one part of the world to another. For example, many people who live in countries close to the equator suffer from malaria (an infectious disease caused by a parasite transmitted in the bite of infected mosquitoes), but malaria is uncommon in cooler countries. Infectious diseases that occur naturally in a country are said to be endemic. At any particular time, a small proportion of the population of a country might be expected to be suffering from an endemic infection.

During the 1918 influenza pandemic, many people, like these soldiers in Seattle, USA, wore masks to try to avoid infection. Unfortunately, the masks were not very effective.

Epidemics and pandemics

If an infection spreads rapidly, affecting more and more people, it is called an epidemic. This can happen when an outbreak of an infectious disease hits a particular town or area. For example, a single case of chickenpox in a school can quickly result in other children in the school becoming infected. The chickenpox can then spread to other schools and other nearby towns.

If an epidemic spreads over a wider area, either within one country or from one country to other countries, eventually affecting a very large number of people, it is said to be a pandemic. For example, in 1916 a pandemic of the disease polio spread across 20 states in the USA and infected nearly 30,000 people, of whom about 7,000 died. The possibility of a pandemic worried many people in 2002, when a few isolated cases of SARS (severe acute respiratory syndrome) in China were rapidly followed by more cases around the world. SARS spreads through coughs and sneezes. Fortunately, although cases were widespread, the numbers infected remained small, and the outbreak did not have serious consequences.

The Black Death

Throughout history, epidemics and pandemics have killed many millions of people. One disease that was particularly feared was bubonic plague. This caused its victims to develop large, black swellings in the armpits and groin. It could kill within a few days. During the fourteenth century, a bubonic plague pandemic, which became known as the Black Death, swept across Asia, North Africa and Europe. In some places it wiped out more than a quarter of the entire population. Less severe plague epidemics occurred at other times – for example, an outbreak of plague occurred in London in 1665, but it was halted by a fire, known as the Great Fire of London, that raged through the city the following year.

CUTTING EDGE — MOMENTS

1918: influenza pandemic

In 1918, just after the end of World War I, another ruthless killer hit the world: influenza. The strain, known as Spanish flu, probably originated in the central USA, and affected around 25 percent of the US population. US soldiers most likely carried it to Europe during World War I, and it then spread rapidly across the globe. Hospitals were overwhelmed by the pandemic and, to cope with the huge numbers of sick people, many governments set up extra wards in school halls and other buildings. However, there was no medicine known that could offer an effective treatment for the illness. Many people also died from secondary bacterial infections that followed influenza infection. By the time the pandemic subsided in 1919, more than 20 million people had died of influenza – a greater number than had been killed during World War I.

This woodcut, from a book published in 1493, shows Christopher Columbus landing on Hispaniola (present-day Haiti) in 1492.

Resistance to disease

Hundreds of years ago, people from one continent had little or no contact with people from other continents. This meant that they were exposed to the infectious diseases that were common in their own lands, but not to those from elsewhere. After exposure to an infection, the body is often able to resist a future attack by the same infection. For example, people who suffer from an infection such as mumps in childhood are unlikely to suffer from mumps a second time – they are said to have built up a resistance, or immunity, to mumps (see panel on page 31 for an explanation of how people develop resistance to diseases).

The higher the proportion of the population that is immune to an infection, the less serious an outbreak of that infection will be, as fewer people will catch it. Only the young, who have not previously been exposed to the infection, and the sick and elderly, who are less able to withstand infections, will succumb to the disease.

When European people began exploring the world and travelling further and further afield, their own particular infectious diseases went along with them. This had serious, sometimes disastrous consequences for the native peoples of the places the Europeans travelled to. Because the diseases were completely new to their immune systems, the native peoples had no resistance to them. Many died as a result of infections such as chickenpox and measles,

CUTTING EDGE FACTS

Sixteenth-century explorers and infectious disease in the Americas

The first contact between Europeans and the peoples of North and South America occurred in the last decade of the fifteenth century. From this time, Christopher Columbus and other explorers began to sail across the Atlantic Ocean, landing in and around the Caribbean. They brought with them many infectious diseases, including smallpox, chickenpox, measles, typhoid, cholera, scarlet fever and influenza. These had never been known in the Americas before, and so the native Americans had no resistance to them. An epidemic that may have been swine fever, an infection usually associated with pigs, swept through Hispaniola in 1493. Serious outbreaks of other infectious diseases followed. Smallpox in particular devastated the native population of Mexico, which fell to one-tenth of its previous level within 50 years of the arrival of the Europeans.

Explorers took the infections with them as they ventured deeper into the Americas. In North America in 1763, British Army officers ordered that blankets that had been exposed to smallpox be given to the natives in order to infect them with the disease. We cannot be certain about the exact number of native people who died from European infections, but some historians estimate that it may have been as many as 90 percent of the population – or nine out of every ten people. This was a tragedy for the native peoples, but made it much easier for the Europeans to conquer their lands.

which were not considered serious by the explorers.

Discovering how diseases spread

People have known that diseases could spread from one person to another for centuries, but it was only during the nineteenth century that scientists began to understand how and why this happened. Through the work of several scientists, including Robert Koch and Louis Pasteur, it was proved that infectious diseases were caused by tiny living things called micro-organisms. This was called the germ theory. Micro-organisms, or microbes, were too small to be seen with the eye and could only be studied using microscopes. Slowly, scientists developed techniques for growing the microbes in the laboratory and studying their life cycles. Scientists began to search for chemicals that could kill microbes and thus cure

CUTTING EDGE   MOMENTS

When were microbes first seen?

Anton van Leeuwenhoek (1632–1723), who lived in Delft, in the Netherlands, was a keen amateur scientist. A textile merchant by trade, he used magnifying lenses to help him inspect the quality of cloth. Using hand-ground lenses, he designed and built several microscopes. He examined drops of rainwater, pond water and well water, as well as scrapings from his own teeth, with one of his microscopes and was very surprised to see tiny things moving around. He thought they looked like tiny animals and so he called them animalcules. Van Leeuwenhoek drew what he saw and sent his drawings to the Royal Society of England in a letter. They were published in the journal of the Royal Society in 1677. This was the first recorded observation of bacteria. It would be almost another two hundred years before scientists proved that these bacteria were the cause of some infectious diseases.

infections. Other scientists searched for ways of preventing a person from developing an infection. This was the origin of the medicines that are standard treatments for many infectious diseases today.

Following the pioneering work by John Snow in the nineteenth century (see panel on page 4), the link between dirty water and some infectious diseases slowly became established and accepted.

Today, the lack of a clean water supply and adequate sanitation still contributes to the spread of infectious diseases such as cholera and typhoid. Although this is of less significance in developed countries, it leads to health problems in many developing countries. Keeping ourselves, our possessions and our surroundings clean and hygienic can help to prevent infections occurring. Hygienic preparation and storage of food is also important in the control of infections such as those that cause food poisoning. For example, storing foods such as meat and milk in a refrigerator rather than at room temperature helps to keep them fresh for longer.

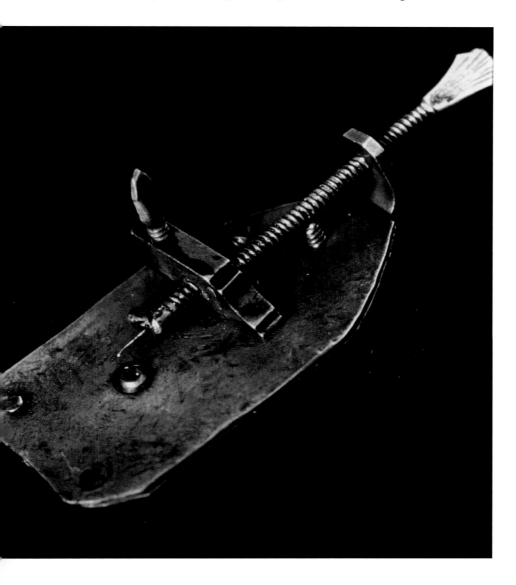

Anton van Leeuwenhoek used this microscope to make the first observations of bacteria more than 300 years ago. The device used a single lens clamped between two brass plates with holes for the viewer to look through. Magnifications of up to 200 times were possible.

CHAPTER 2

Pathogens and Infectious Diseases

Anything that causes an infectious disease is known as a pathogen. Many pathogens are micro-organisms, but some pathogens are larger organisms. Pathogens can be divided into four main groups: bacteria, viruses, fungi and parasites. When a pathogen enters the body, it triggers a reaction by the body's defence systems (see panel on page 31). In many cases, the pathogen is detected and destroyed before it causes any harm. In some cases, though, it multiplies very quickly and the body's defences cannot destroy it before its effects are felt.

Bacteria

There are probably more bacteria on Earth than any other type of organism. We have bacteria living in our intestines, on our skin and on every surface around us. Some bacteria are good for us, such as those that live in the intestines and help in the process of digestion. Others, however, are responsible for a wide range of infectious diseases.

Bacteria are single-celled organisms. Some are rod-shaped, some are spherical and some are spiral. Some have tiny hair-like structures called flagellae that can flick, helping the bacterium to move. Although there are many different types of bacteria, they all have some basic similarities. Most are less than 0.001 mm long.

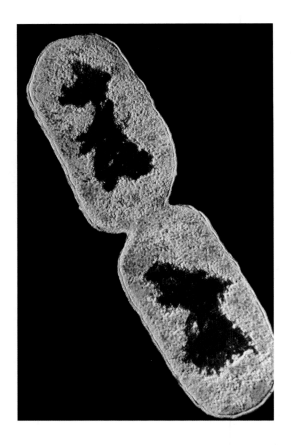

This micrograph (a photo of an image seen through a microscope) shows two cells of *Escherichia coli*, a rod-shaped bacterium that can cause digestive system infections.

They have a complex outer layer called a cell wall, made from a mixture of proteins, sugars and fats. Inside the bacterium, a jelly-like liquid called the cytoplasm often contains granules that provide food for the cell.

Bacterial cells differ in important ways from animal cells. Animal cells contain their genetic information in material called chromatin in the nucleus. During cell division, the chromatin forms thread-like structures called chromosomes. These structures carry the genetic information from one generation to the next. Bacterial cells do not have a nucleus. Instead, the chromosome is just curled up in the cytoplasm. Some bacteria also contain one or more much smaller circular strands of genetic material, called plasmids.

Most bacteria feed by releasing digestive enzymes. These are proteins that break down food outside the bacterium. The bacteria can then absorb the nutrients that have been released. Each bacterium produces waste products, called toxins, which are released. In many bacterial infections it is the toxins rather than the bacteria themselves that make people ill.

CUTTING EDGE — SCIENCE

Multiplying bacteria
This diagram makes it is easier to understand what happens when a single bacterium divides.

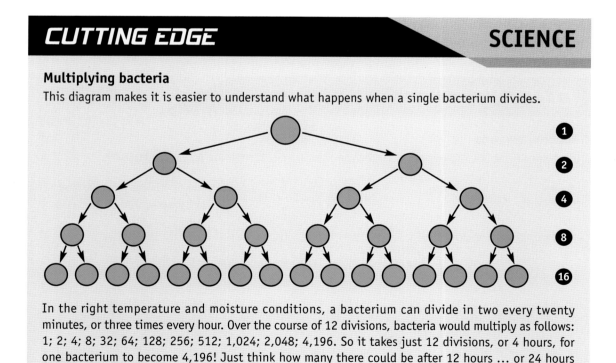

In the right temperature and moisture conditions, a bacterium can divide in two every twenty minutes, or three times every hour. Over the course of 12 divisions, bacteria would multiply as follows: 1; 2; 4; 8; 32; 64; 128; 256; 512; 1,024; 2,048; 4,196. So it takes just 12 divisions, or 4 hours, for one bacterium to become 4,196! Just think how many there could be after 12 hours ... or 24 hours ... or 2 days!

Bacteria have a very simple life cycle. A bacterium simply grows bigger until it is too big to exist as one cell. It then splits into two to make two new bacteria. This process of division is called fission. Each of the new bacteria cells grows and then divides into two, and each of these in turn grows and divides into two, and so on. The group of bacteria that develops is known as a colony.

There are many different types of bacteria, causing many different infections. Bacteria are responsible for abscesses and boils (infected pores in the skin), sore throats, food poisoning and septic (infected) wounds, as well as life-threatening diseases. Some of the best-known infectious diseases caused by bacteria include:

Tuberculosis (TB) Tuberculosis is an infectious disease caused by the bacterium *Mycobacterium tuberculosis*, which affects nearly one third of the world's population. In developed countries, the usual site of infection is the lungs, while in parts of Africa abdominal tuberculosis is also common. Other parts of the body may also be affected. As the bacteria multiply, they damage small areas of lung tissue. At this stage the infection is not serious. However, the infection may spread throughout the lungs, leading to breathing difficulties and, if untreated, eventual death.

CUTTING EDGE   SCIENCE

Naming bacteria
Bacteria can be put into groups according to their shape. Each group has a special name.

name	shape	example of illness or condition caused by each type of bacteria
Coccus	spherical a) in chains – *Streptococcus* b) in clusters – *Staphylococcus* c) in pairs – *Gonococci*	scarlet fever abscesses gonorrhoea
Bacillus	rod-shaped	typhoid
Vibrio	bent rod-shaped	cholera
Spirilla (or Spirochaetes)	spiral	syphilis

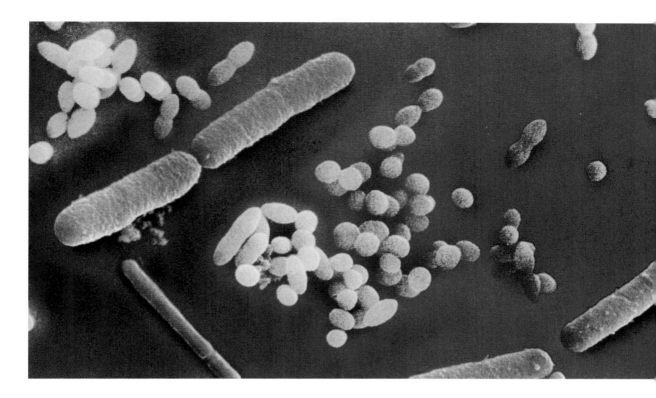

Typhoid Typhoid is caused by a bacterium called *Salmonella typhi* that infects the intestines. Bacteria leave the body in the faeces. In places where clean water is unavailable and sanitation is poor, food and water may become contaminated by faeces, spreading the infection to other people. At first, typhoid causes flu-like symptoms, followed by abdominal pain, diarrhoea and a rash. Without treatment, dehydration (too little water in the body) can become severe and the infection may be fatal.

This micrograph shows rod-shaped and spherical bacteria found in the human gut. The rod-shaped bacteria are bacilli. The ball-shaped bacteria are cocci.

Cholera Cholera is an infection of the intestine by the bacterium *Vibrio cholerae*. It leads to vomiting and diarrhoea, which in turn lead to severe dehydration and death. Cholera is spread via faeces and contaminated water and is therefore a particular problem in areas without adequate sanitation and clean water supplies.

Tetanus Tetanus is caused by the bacterium *Clostridium tetani* that occurs in soil. The bacteria enter the body via a wound in the skin. As they multiply they produce a toxin that paralyses first the jaw muscles and then other muscles.

Bacterial meningitis This is caused by infection of the fluid that surrounds the brain and spinal cord by a *Meningococcus* bacterium. The infection irritates the meninges (membranes surrounding the brain) and they become swollen. Meningitis spreads from one person to another via coughs and sneezes. The illness may begin very suddenly with headache, sore neck and fever, or may develop more slowly over several days. As the bacteria multiply they can infect the blood and spread throughout the body causing a skin rash. Bacterial meningitis is rare in most developed countries but is a major killer in some parts of the world, especially in West Africa.

Viruses

Most viruses are many times smaller than bacteria. There is a wide variety of shape and structure but they all have a protein coat, called a capsule, enclosing a central core of genetic material. Viruses are not really complete cells as they have no nucleus, cytoplasm or cell membrane. They do not carry out basic life processes such as growing, feeding, respiration or getting rid of waste products, and they are unable to reproduce without a host cell. For these reasons they are called particles rather than cells.

Viruses can survive on their own, but they must be inside another living cell (a host cell) in order to reproduce. In most cases the virus particle sticks to the host cell membrane. Either the virus's

CUTTING EDGE   MOMENTS

The first electron microscopes

In the 1930s, more advanced microscopes were developed, enabling scientists to study viruses for the first time. Before this, all microscopes worked by shining a beam of light onto or through the object that scientists wanted to study. The maximum magnification that could be achieved with this type of microscope was about x 2,000 – not enough to show details of structures inside cells.

Then, in 1932, two German scientists called Max Knoll and Ernest Ruska developed a new type of microscope: a transmission electron microscope. Instead of using a beam of light, it shone a beam of electrons through the material being studied. Although their first instrument could only magnify x 17, the technology was refined and developed rapidly, eventually providing sufficient magnification to allow scientists to see inside cells in detail – and to see the structure of viruses for the first time.

In 1952, Sir Charles Oatley, an English scientist, developed a scanning electron microscope. This shone a beam of electrons at the surface of an object to produce a three-dimensional image. Modern electron microscopes can magnify objects more than two million times!

genetic material or the complete virus particle then enters the host cell. Once inside the host cell, the virus's genetic material hijacks the cell's mechanisms. It stops the cell from carrying out its normal processes and makes it produce lots of copies of the virus's genetic material and capsules. These are then assembled to make new virus particles, which escape from the cell and infect other host cells – and the whole process begins again. The host cells are destroyed by the virus particles, and it is this destruction that leads to the symptoms of the disease caused by each virus.

In this micrograph you can see a vaccinia virus particle (pink) inside a human cell (yellow). The vaccinia virus causes cowpox, a disease of cattle and humans.

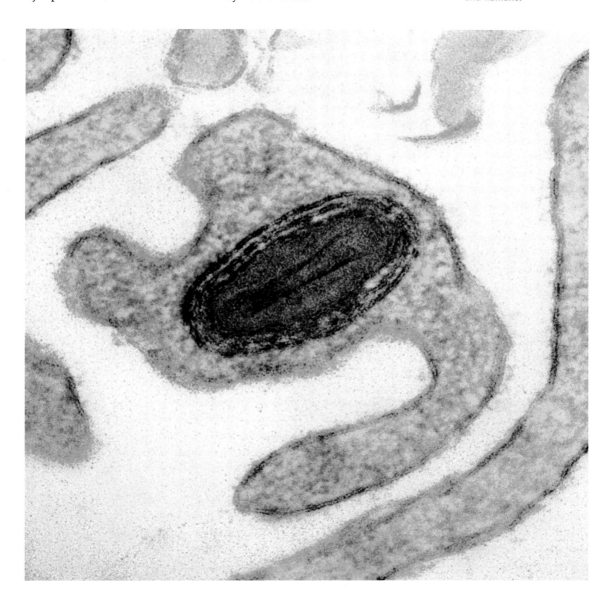

There are many different types of virus, causing a multitude of infections. Viruses are responsible for colds and flu, warts, verrucas (warts that grow on the foot) and childhood diseases such as chickenpox, as well as life-threatening diseases. Two viral infections that have received much publicity in recent years are HIV/AIDS and SARS.

HIV/AIDS The first recorded case of HIV/AIDS occurred in 1981. It is caused by the Human Immunodeficiency Virus (HIV), which attacks the body's immune system. A person who is infected with HIV is said to be HIV positive. Eventually, HIV weakens the immune system so much that the person becomes ill with other infections. It is at this stage that a person is said to have AIDS (Acquired Immune Deficiency Syndrome). HIV/AIDS is spread during sexual intercourse from an infected person to a non-infected person, and in many countries people are advised to use a condom to reduce the risk of becoming infected. HIV/AIDS can also be spread in infected blood, for example among drug users sharing non-sterile hypodermic needles. HIV/AIDS is a serious global pandemic – there were 3.1 million AIDS-related deaths in 2005, and some scientists predict that by 2010, about 85 million people worldwide will be HIV positive.

CUTTING EDGE — SCIENTISTS

David Ho, virologist

David Ho was born on 3 November 1952 in Taiwan. His family moved to the USA and settled in Los Angeles. Because David spoke no English, he found school lessons very difficult at first, but he quickly learned the language. He studied physics at Massachusetts Institute of Technology and California Institute of Technology, but switched to molecular biology and won a scholarship to Harvard Medical School. There, he saw some of the first cases of AIDS and decided that this would be the focus of his work. David began to search for ways of combating the infection at its earliest stages. He devised the 'cocktails' (mixtures) of antiviral drugs that are now widely used in the treatment of AIDS. In his current research he continues to look for improved treatments and for an AIDS vaccine. David Ho was appointed Director of the Aaron Diamond AIDS Research Center in New York City, and in 1996 he was named as *Time* magazine's Man of the Year.

SARS SARS stands for Severe Acute Respiratory Syndrome and is caused by a virus similar to the virus responsible for the common cold. The virus infects the lungs, where it causes severe damage. It spreads rapidly from an infected person to others in close contact with them, through coughs and sneezes. Worldwide panic followed a SARS outbreak in 2002. International travel carried the virus around the world. In many countries, anyone showing SARS-like symptoms and any people who had been in physical contact with them were quarantined (kept away from others) until the outbreak was brought under control.

In this micrograph, particles of the HIV virus (red) have infected a lymphocyte (green) – a type of white blood cell.

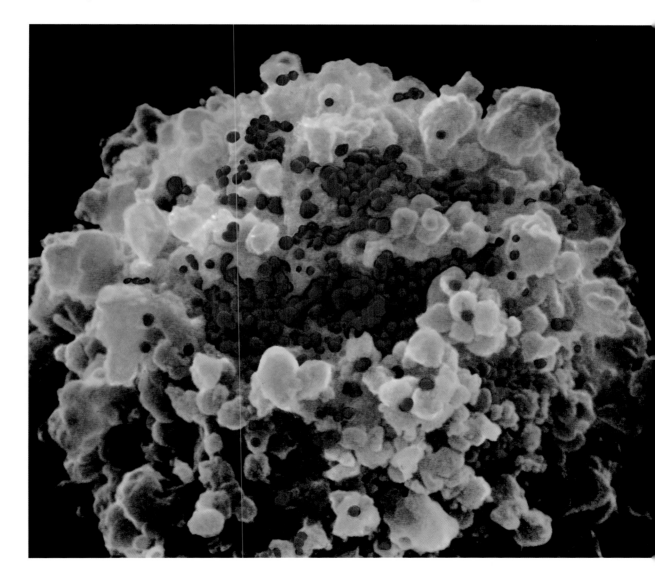

Fungi

Fungi are made up from long threads called hyphae (singular: hypha). These are similar to cells, as they have an outer wall and cytoplasm, with a space, or vacuole, at the centre. Unlike other cells, though, their nuclei are spread throughout the cytoplasm. The hyphae form a network called a mycelium that spreads throughout the material on which the hyphae are growing. Fungi absorb food from the material they are growing on. Most reproduce by releasing tiny cells called spores from special hyphae called fruiting bodies. The spores then germinate (begin to grow) to form a new mycelium.

Some fungi cause infectious diseases in plants, while others affect animals. There are more than 75,000 known species of fungi, but only about 200 cause infections in humans. Most fungal infections affect the skin rather than internal organs, and many affect people whose bodies are already weakened from another illness or some other cause.

CUTTING EDGE · FACTS

Useful fungi

Not all fungi are bad news! Some, such as yeast, are useful. We use yeasts to make bread. Yeasts are also used to ferment sugar to make wine and beer. Other fungi are used to turn milk into yoghurt. The mushrooms that we eat are also fungi. The first antibiotic chemicals were extracted from fungi and many antibiotics today are still derived from them.

Thrush Thrush is a common human fungal infection caused by the fungus *Candida albicans*. It usually affects the mouth or vagina, although it can also affect other parts of the body. In the mouth, white patches appear on the gums, lips and inside of the cheeks. In the vagina, thrush causes a white discharge. *Candida albicans* is present in a healthy digestive system and does not normally cause any problems. Thrush can flare up elsewhere in the body for several reasons including pregnancy, diabetes, use of oral contraceptives, use of antibiotics or wearing tight, nylon clothing.

Athlete's foot and ringworm Another common type of fungal infection causes conditions that have different names depending on which part of the body is affected. In athlete's foot, the mycelium of the fungus *Trichophyton* grows on the skin between the toes and is spread easily to another person via contaminated towels, floors and clothing. Athlete's foot is common among people with sweaty feet and among those who do not dry their feet thoroughly after bathing or swimming.

Ringworm is caused by a similar fungus, *Microsporum*, on the scalp. Ringworm gets its name from the circular rings that appear on the scalp. As the fungus grows outwards, it dies at the centre, creating a red itchy ring that gradually increases in size. Another fungus, *Epidermophyton*, causes ringworm in the groin. Each of these fungi grow best in warm, damp conditions and usually spread by direct contact with an infected person.

This micrograph shows the infection of a human nail with athlete's foot. The red structures are spores from the fungus *Tricophyton*.

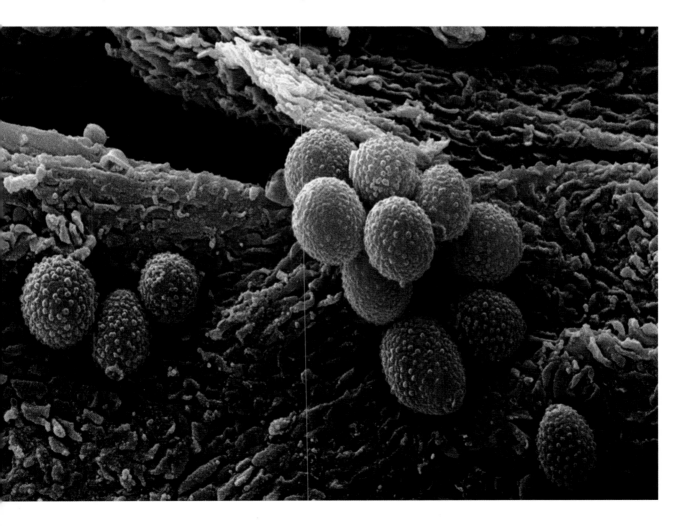

Parasites

Organisms that live off another living organism and damage it are called parasites. Humans and other animals can be infected by a wide range of parasites, both common and rare. Different parasites thrive in different conditions and so they vary around the world depending on the climate.

Some parasites are single-celled organisms called protozoa. They have a cell membrane, cytoplasm and a nucleus. Some have long hair-like structures called flagellae that help them to move around. Protozoa multiply by dividing, like bacteria, or by 'budding', a process in which small outgrowths of the cell swell and then break off to form new cells. Protozoa can survive cold and dry conditions outside a host by forming cysts, structures that lie dormant (in an inactive state) but which develop into new protozoan cells when they re-enter a host.

Some parasites are larger, multi-celled organisms. Fleas and lice, for example, are parasites that live on the surface of the body and feed on the host's blood. Other parasites, such as liver flukes (flatworms that infest the liver), live inside the host's body and feed directly on the host's blood or body tissues.

CUTTING EDGE — FACTS

Discovering words

Knowing the origins of words can help us to understand their meaning or give us extra information:

pathogen comes from two Greek words:
pathos – suffering
genes – to give rise to
Most pathogens do cause suffering.

parasite comes from two Greek words:
para – beside
sitos – food
So, parasites live 'beside their food' – or even in it!

protozoa comes from two Greek words:
proto – first
zoa – animal
Protozoans are thought to be like the very first animals that developed on Earth.

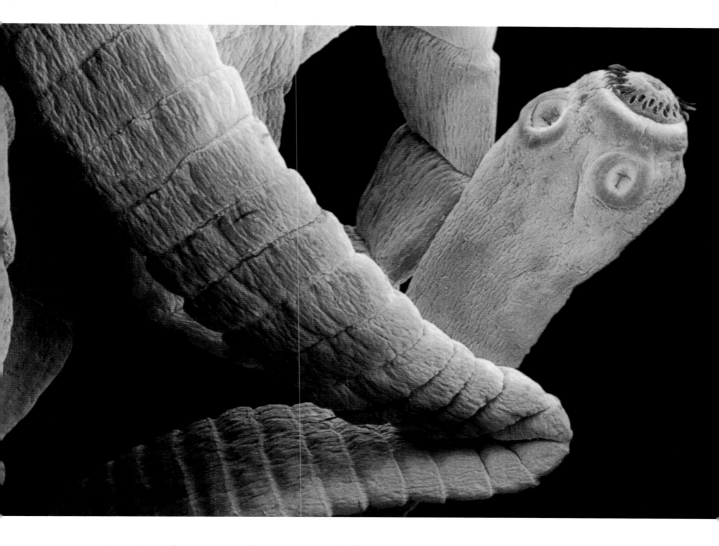

Parasite infections can be spread easily from person to person. Many parasites produce eggs that leave the body in the faeces. If hygiene and sanitation is poor – for example if drinking water becomes contaminated by human waste – these eggs can get into other people. The eggs mature into adult parasites, which produce more eggs, and so the cycle continues. Some parasites, such as those responsible for malaria and sleeping sickness, rely on insects to spread them to a new host. Insects used in this way are called vectors. Some parasites, such as tapeworms, spend part of their life cycle living in other animals such as cows or pigs. The eggs of these parasites are transferred to people when people eat the meat of an infected animal.

In this micrograph of a tapeworm, you can see the head with suckers and hooklets that it uses to anchor itself to the inside of the host's intestines.

Parasites are responsible for many different infectious diseases. These include:

Malaria Malaria is caused by the protozoa *Plasmodium* and spreads via an insect vector. When a mosquito bites and sucks the blood of an infected person, it picks up the protozoa. The infection is then passed on when the mosquito bites another person. Most cases of malaria occur in the tropical areas of the world. Malaria causes fever and vomiting and, if not treated, may result in kidney and liver damage and eventually death.

CUTTING EDGE　　SCIENCE

Malaria and sickle cell anaemia

Sickle cell anaemia is an illness that is common in the same areas of the world as malaria. It causes red blood cells to become distorted and carry oxygen around the body less efficiently than in healthy people. It is an inherited condition – passed from one generation to the next. To develop the full condition, an individual must inherit two copies of the sickle cell gene, one from each parent. People who inherit a sickle cell gene from one parent and a normal gene from the other develop a milder condition called sickle cell trait. Scientists have discovered that people with sickle cell trait are less likely to suffer from malaria than other people. This is because the malaria parasite, which spends part of its life cycle living in red blood cells, cannot survive in sickled red blood cells, because they rupture and prevent the parasite from reproducing. Also, the protein in red blood cells that transports oxygen around the body is different in sickled cells and the malaria parasite cannot digest it. It is therefore difficult for the malaria parasite to survive in people with sickle cell trait. This is why sickle cell trait offers some protection against malaria.

Sleeping sickness This disease occurs mainly in Africa. It is caused by the protozoa *Trypanosoma*, which infects the blood and brain and damages the nervous system. The infection is spread from person to person via an insect vector, the tsetse fly.

Schistosomiasis Schistosomiasis, also known as bilharzia, is caused by a parasitic flatworm, *Schistosoma*. It occurs mainly in tropical areas. The infection is spread in the form of eggs via faeces or urine

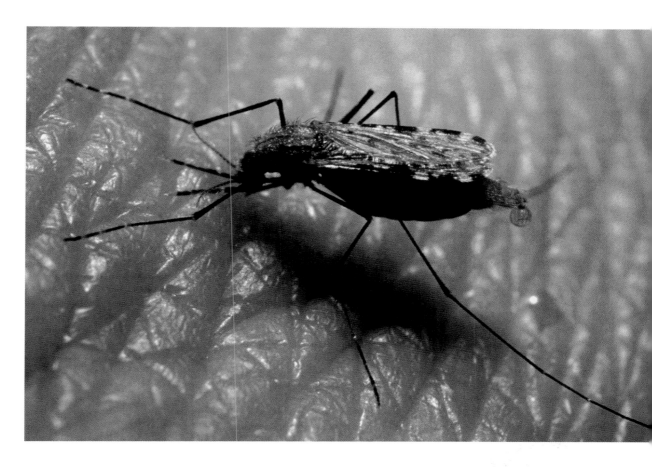

from infected people. The eggs then develop inside freshwater snails and are released as larvae. These penetrate the skin of people who bathe in the infected water. Once inside the body, the larvae infect blood vessels in the intestine. Schistomosiasis causes diarrhoea and liver damage and, if not treated, may be fatal.

Tapeworms There are several different types of tapeworm, but the most common is the beef tapeworm, *Taenia saginata*. It is spread via eggs in faeces from an infected person. When the eggs are eaten by another animal, such as a cow, they hatch into larvae and infect the muscles. The larvae spread to another person when the person eats the meat of the animal. The tapeworm attaches itself to the intestine and absorbs nutrients from food passing through the digestive system. The person may lose weight and become weak due to lack of nutrients. Cooking meat thoroughly kills the tapeworm larvae and so the infection is not passed on.

This mosquito is seen biting human skin and feeding on blood. The protozoa that cause malaria are passed on via the mosquito's saliva.

How do pathogens get into the body?

There are millions of micro-organisms and other pathogens around us! Very few of the things that we handle every day will be completely free from pathogens, and the body's first line of defence against them is the skin. This waterproof outer layer acts as a barrier that pathogens such as bacteria and viruses cannot penetrate. If the skin is damaged, for example from a cut, dirt and micro-organisms may get into the body via the damaged area. They may cause a localized infection (an infection that affects a small part of the body) or, if the micro-organisms enter the bloodstream, they may cause a widespread infection often called blood poisoning or septicaemia.

Another entry route for pathogens is via our food and drink. If foods are not properly stored, prepared or cooked, they may contain pathogens that we take into our bodies when we eat. Some,

Here you can see a cluster of *Staphylococcus* bacteria (yellow) among the tiny hairs (blue) that line the human airways. This type of bacteria causes diseases ranging from minor skin infections to serious illnesses such as pneumonia.

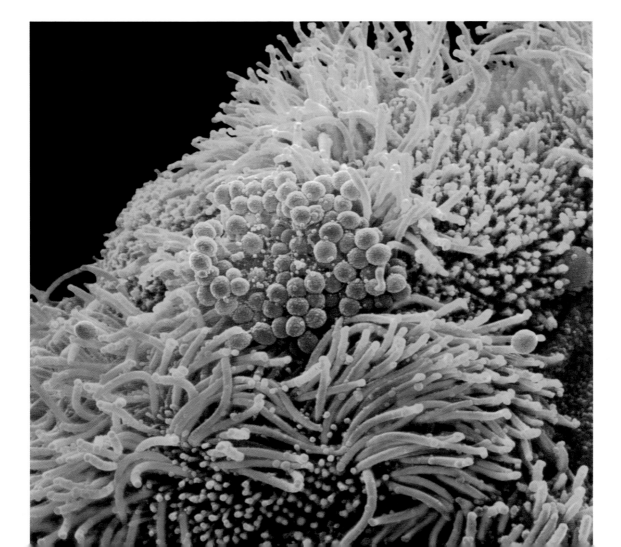

such as the bacterium *Listeria monocytogenes*, multiply in the food and continue to multiply in the digestive system. Others, such as the bacterium *Clostridium botulinum*, produce toxins that accumulate in the food. Both the micro-organisms and the toxins cause an illness known as food poisoning. The symptoms are abdominal pain, diarrhoea and vomiting.

A third entry route for pathogens is via the airways. Micro-organisms in the air enter the airways and travel to the lungs when we breathe in. Tiny hairs line the nasal cavity and the airways, trapping some dirt and microbes. However, some micro-organisms evade this defence and, when they reach a part of the body that provides the conditions which they need to live, they multiply. This can cause localized infections such as tonsillitis, or 'strep throat'. Micro-organisms can also cause more serious infections such as bronchitis, pneumonia and tuberculosis.

Some micro-organisms are passed from one person to another via medical processes such as blood transfusions. Today, extensive testing on all blood products helps ensure that infections will not be passed on by such procedures.

Some micro-organisms, such as the HIV virus, are very fragile and can only survive outside a host for a minute or two. Others are more robust and can survive outside a host for longer periods. For example, *Escherichia coli*, a bacterium that causes food poisoning, can survive for up to 24 hours outside a host. Some micro-organisms can survive outside a host, often as spores (a dormant stage in the micro-organism's life cycle), for many years.

CUTTING EDGE   FACTS

Anthrax survival

During World War II, the British government investigated what would happen if anthrax spores were used as a biological weapon. They exploded a bomb filled with anthrax spores on the Scottish island of Gruinard, and within a few days the sheep on the island began to die. Because anthrax spores can survive in the soil, the island was quarantined and no one was allowed to visit. It was not until 1990, 48 years after the anthrax was released, that the island was declared anthrax-free and the quarantine order was lifted.

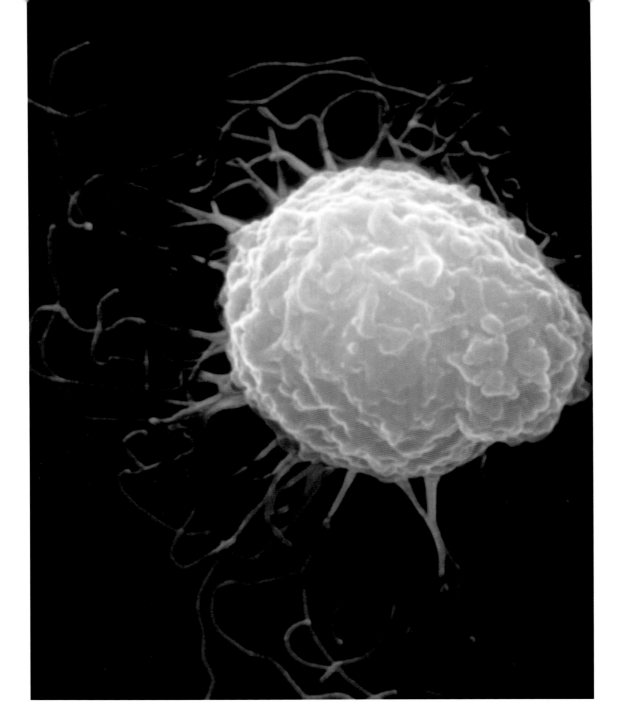

How does the body react to micro-organisms?

Many micro-organisms live in and on the human body without causing any harm. Some, like intestinal bacteria that help in the process of digestion, can actually be beneficial. The body just ignores these. Other micro-organisms can make us ill, so the body has an in-built set of reactions to get rid of them as quickly as possible.

White blood cells like the one seen in this micrograph are part of the body's immune system.

Blood oozing out of cut skin carries micro-organisms away from the site of the injury. Blood cells flood into the area to repair the damage and, at the same time, destroy any micro-organisms that have entered the body. A scab quickly forms over the damaged area, acting as a protective layer until the skin below heals. This helps to prevent any other micro-organisms from entering through the damaged area.

Food that contains micro-organisms often looks or smells unpleasant and so we avoid eating it. However, if we do eat food that contains harmful micro-organisms or toxins, the body often expels it rapidly by vomiting. It can also flush it through the digestive system very quickly. Although vomiting and diarrhoea are not pleasant, they do expel micro-organisms quickly.

Micro-organisms that enter the airways often cause irritation, which makes the body produce mucus or phlegm. When we cough or sneeze to expel the mucus and phlegm, we also expel micro-organisms.

Tears contain a natural antibiotic called lysozyme. If an eye becomes infected, tears are produced that help to wash the micro-organisms away. The lysozyme in the tears helps to kill any bacteria that remain.

Some micro-organisms evade all of these defences, though. The body's immune system is then activated and a major attack on the micro-organisms begins.

CUTTING EDGE   SCIENCE

The immune response and micro-organisms

The body's attack on micro-organisms involves many different organs and tissues. Together, these make up the immune system, and the attack on the micro-organisms is called an immune response. The cells that actually attack the micro-organisms are the white blood cells. As soon as an infection is detected, the body rapidly produces extra white blood cells. Some white blood cells, called phagocytes, engulf the micro-organisms and destroy them. Others produce special chemicals called antibodies that stick to the surface of the micro-organisms, making them easier for the phagocytes to target and destroy. Some white blood cells 'remember' the micro-organism so that if it ever enters the body again, the immune system will recognize it and react very quickly. This is how people develop a resistance to a disease.

CHAPTER 3

Treating Infectious Diseases

There are four main ways in which we can treat infectious diseases or prevent them from occurring. One method is to use medicines that attack pathogens, such as antibiotics and antiviral drugs. Another method is vaccination. Vaccines can be given to protect the body and prevent a disease from developing. The third method is hygiene. High standards of cleanliness can prevent some infections occurring. Finally, there are many natural remedies that can help to boost the immune system. Different infections require different treatments.

Antibiotics

Antibiotics are chemicals that attack bacteria. They have no effect on viruses or fungi and are therefore only useful in the treatment of infections caused by bacteria and some parasites. Although many people ask for antibiotics to treat a cold or influenza, there is no point in a doctor prescribing them for such conditions: antibiotics cannot cure viral infections.

Antibiotics can be taken by mouth as tablets or capsules. Some antibiotic creams and lotions are also available for treating skin infections. In severe infections, antibiotics may be given by an intravenous drip system. In this method, an antibiotic solution travels through a tube straight into the patient's bloodstream.

CUTTING EDGE MOMENTS

The discovery of the antibiotic penicillin

The discovery of penicillin came about almost by accident. In 1928, an English scientist, Alexander Fleming, was studying an enzyme called lysozyme. He left some culture dishes in his laboratory while he went away for a few days. When he got back, he found that one of the dishes contained a patch of mould, along with some microbes that had begun to grow but had then died. He grew some more of the mould and tested it. He found it produced a chemical that could kill other microbes. The mould was called *Penicillium notatum* and so Fleming decided to call the chemical 'penicillin'.

The amount of antibiotic being given can be monitored and adjusted as the patient's condition worsens or improves.

Some antibiotics kill bacteria while others prevent them from multiplying, allowing the immune system to destroy them. Antibiotics that are effective against a wide range of bacteria are known as broad-spectrum antibiotics. These may be used when a patient is so seriously ill that treatment needs to begin before the specific bacterium causing the infection has been identified. They are also used when a patient has an infection caused by several different types of bacteria. Other antibiotics, which are only effective against a limited range of bacteria, are known as narrow-spectrum antibiotics. They are useful when the specific bacterium responsible for the infection is known.

Alexander Fleming, the discoverer of penicillin, in his laboratory.

CUTTING EDGE SCIENCE

How do antibiotics kill micro-organisms?
Some antibiotics damage the bacterial cell wall so that the bacteria slowly become leaky and die. Some antibiotics stop the bacteria from making new protein molecules, thus preventing them from functioning normally. Other antibiotics stop the bacteria from dividing properly. This means that no more bacteria can be produced and any bacteria that die cannot be replaced.

Some of the first antibiotics used in the treatment of bacterial infections were a group of medicines known as sulfa drugs, developed in the 1930s. These drugs, created from chemical dyes, killed bacteria. Although sulfa drugs were important during World War II, they caused unpleasant side effects such as sickness and fever. The first antibiotic suitable for general use was penicillin. Commercial production of penicillin began during World War II, when it was used to treat injured soldiers. Soon after the war, it was made available to the wider public. Scientists began to search for other antibiotic chemicals, and during the 1950s and 1960s, many new antibiotics were introduced.

Today, doctors have access to a large number of antibiotics. Different antibiotics are used to treat different types of bacterial infection. When antibiotics are prescribed, it is important that the patient finishes the course of treatment. If he or she stops taking the antibiotics too soon, some bacteria may survive and multiply; if this happens, the infection can break out again.

Antiviral drugs

Viruses are very small and will only grow inside other cells, so it has been more difficult to develop antiviral drugs than antibiotics. The first antiviral drugs were developed during the 1960s, but were only available for a few specific viruses. Since the 1980s, many more antiviral drugs have become available. This has been possible because modern techniques have helped scientists to learn and understand more about viruses and how they behave.

Different antiviral drugs work in different ways. Some are specific to a single virus. For example, amantadine is effective against some strains of influenza virus. It works by preventing virus particles from getting into host cells. Zidovudine (AZT),which is effective against HIV, prevents the virus's genetic material being copied. Other antiviral drugs, also specific to a single virus, work by preventing new virus particles being assembled or by preventing the release of the new virus particles from the host cell.

An alternative approach is to stimulate the body's own immune response to the virus particles. Some antiviral drugs, such as interferons, are effective against a range of viruses. They work indirectly by stimulating the body's immune system to attack the virus particles. Antibodies can also be used to stick to the virus particles and thus highlight them as targets for the immune system to attack.

This micrograph shows crystals of ampicillin, an antibiotic used to treat infections such as bronchitis and typhoid.

Antifungal medicines

Fungal infections can be treated in a variety of ways. Most antifungal treatments work by damaging the fungal wall (see page 22), which kills the fungus. Antifungal creams, known as topical antifungals, can be put onto the surface of the infected area. Shampoos containing antifungal chemicals can be used to wash the hair if the scalp is infected. To treat some fungal infections, antifungal medicines can be taken by mouth or given by injection.

CUTTING EDGE — SCIENCE

How do antifungal drugs work?

Because fungi are similar in many ways to animal cells, many potential treatments that would kill fungi will also harm the patient's own cells. To avoid this, antifungal medicines must target the few differences that exist between animal and fungal cells. Some work by attaching to specific chemicals in the fungal wall, making the wall leaky and thus killing the fungus. Other antifungal medicines work by preventing these cell wall chemicals from being produced. Human cells do not contain the cell wall chemicals and so the patient is not harmed.

Treating parasitic infections

Simple precautions can be taken to avoid contracting parasitic infections in the first place. Different precautions are appropriate, depending on the parasites that are found in the local environment. They include the following:

malaria Use a mosquito net at night to avoid being bitten by malaria-carrying mosquitos; also, some drugs can be taken to prevent an infection from developing.

schistosomiasis Avoid contact with infected water.

tapeworms Cook all meat thoroughly.

Prevention and treatment of parasitic infections differ, depending on the cause of the infection. Several different methods are available.

Bark from this plant, *Cinchona succirubra*, was an original source of the anti-malarial drug quinine.

medicines One of the oldest medicines to combat parasitic infections is quinine, which has been used for centuries to treat malaria. Quinine was traditionally made from the powdered bark of a South American tree, but it can now be synthesized (made in a laboratory) and manufactured commercially. Medicines like this, which kill the parasite inside the body, cure the infection in the person who takes the medicine and also prevent the infection from being passed on to others.

vaccines Vaccines contain a small amount of dead or weakened infectious material. By introducing this into the body, the vaccine primes the body's immune system to mount a defence against that organism in the future. If a big enough proportion of the population is vaccinated, the disease will be brought under control and eventually die out.

insect control One way to contain the spread of a parasitic infection is to reduce the number of insect vectors by, for example, the use of insecticides. Insect repellent chemicals, available in different forms such as gels, sprays and creams, can help to keep insects away.

clean water The provision of clean drinking water and improved sanitation can reduce the incidence (frequency) and spread of water-related infections such as schistomosiasis.

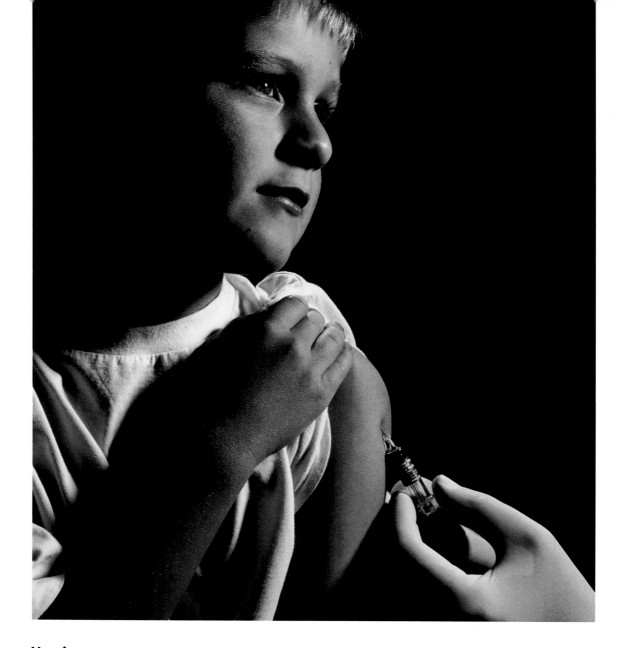

Vaccines

Vaccines are useful in the fight against infectious diseases because they prevent an infection from developing. When a person is vaccinated, a small amount of dead or weakened micro-organism is injected into the person's body. This cannot cause an infection, but the person's immune system is alerted to the presence of 'foreign' material. Some white blood cells 'remember' the characteristics of the micro-organism. If the same micro-organism enters the body again, the immune system will recognize it and respond very quickly, destroying it before an infection has time to develop. For some micro-

A medical worker gives this boy a tetanus booster injection.

organisms, such as measles, a vaccination offers protection that lasts throughout a person's lifetime. For others, such as tetanus, the protection gradually becomes less effective and another injection, known as a 'booster', is necessary every few years.

Smallpox is a good example of the effectiveness of vaccination. Before vaccination was introduced worldwide, smallpox was a major killer. Following the introduction of a mass vaccination programme by the World Health Organisation in 1967, the last recorded case of smallpox was in 1977, and by 1980 smallpox was declared officially eradicated (wiped out) worldwide. Now, only a few samples of the smallpox bacterium remain, kept under high security in special laboratories.

Vaccination has also been very successful against a disease called polio. This caused muscle paralysis in many children and, if it affected the muscles of the chest, could cause death by preventing the child from breathing. In 1952 there were more than 58,000 cases of polio in the United States. After the introduction of a polio vaccine in 1954 , the number of cases dropped rapidly and, by the end of the decade, there were fewer than ten cases a year in the USA. In 1994, the Americas were officially declared polio-free. Today, polio still occurs in India, Pakistan and parts of Africa.

CUTTING EDGE   MOMENTS

The first vaccination

The first recorded vaccination was carried out in 1796 by Edward Jenner, a doctor from Gloucestershire, England. Smallpox was an infectious disease that killed many people and left others badly scarred. It was generally understood in the countryside that dairy maids, who often caught a related but milder disease called cowpox, were much less likely to catch smallpox than other people. Jenner thought that the cowpox might be giving them some protection against smallpox. To test his theory, he took some cowpox pus from a dairymaid and scratched it into the arm of a healthy young boy. The boy caught cowpox and recovered. A few weeks later, Jenner repeated the process – but this time he used the deadly smallpox pus. The boy did not catch smallpox. Jenner's idea worked: by exposing people to cowpox, he could protect them against smallpox. His method became known as vaccination, after the latin word for cow, *vacca*.

Hygiene

Keeping ourselves, our clothes, our possessions, our food and our surroundings hygienic can significantly reduce the likelihood of catching an infectious disease. For most people in developed countries, this is not too difficult. However, in some parts of the world where there is no clean water supply and inadequate sanitation, this can be extremely difficult.

Regular washing, showering or bathing gets rid of micro-organisms from the surface of the skin. Personal hygiene when using the toilet is very important – many micro-organisms leave the body in faeces and can easily be transferred to the hands. These micro-organisms can be removed by washing the hands thoroughly with soap. If hand-washing is inadequate, the micro-organisms can be transferred to other surfaces such as towels and handles, and from there to other people. Infections can spread rapidly in this way.

Cleaning wounds thoroughly minimizes the risk of micro-organisms entering the body via the damaged skin and causing an infection. Many modern products are available to assist in this, such as antiseptic wipes, sprays and creams. Using a sterile dressing such as a plaster to cover the wound and keep it clean provides a barrier to micro-organisms until the skin below has healed.

Storing and preparing food hygienically, and cooking it thoroughly, can reduce the risk of contracting an infection from

CUTTING EDGE MOMENTS

Introduction of antiseptics

It was not until the late nineteenth century that people began to understand the link between cleanliness and infectious disease. At that time, many people who went to a hospital for treatment died of infections. Joseph Lister (1827–1912) was a Scottish surgeon who pioneered the introduction of effective hygiene in hospitals from the mid-1860s onwards. The first chemical he used to combat infection was carbolic acid. Lister arranged for it to be sprayed in the operating theatres during operations, and he even used it directly on dressings for patients' wounds. The infection rates in Lister's hospital dropped rapidly. Slowly, other doctors took up his ideas. Dirty wounds that become infected are said to be septic, and so the chemicals that were developed to combat this became known as antiseptics.

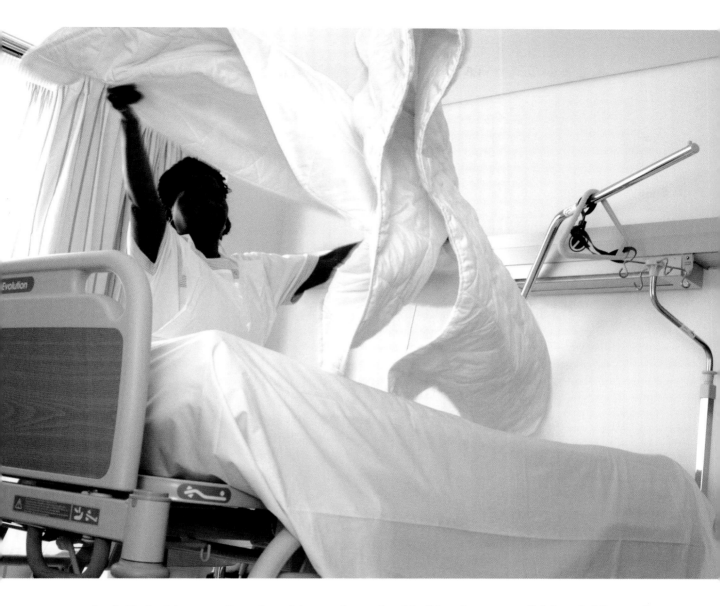

food. To do this, utensils and working surfaces should all be clean. Food should be stored, prepared and cooked following the instructions on the packaging.

Hygiene in hospitals is very important to prevent infections from spreading from patient to patient. This is accomplished by a variety of standard procedures, such as frequent hand-washing by medical staff and the use of sterile (free of micro-organisms) instruments and dressings. If a patient does develop an infection, he or she may be isolated to prevent the infection from spreading.

To help control the spread of infection, hospital linen is removed after use by a patient and is thoroughly cleaned before being reused.

Natural remedies

Many people feel that there must be a better way to combat infectious diseases than waiting until an infection has developed and then using antibiotics or antiviral drugs to treat it. Preventing the infection from developing in the first place would be ideal. Vaccines can do this for many diseases. Other methods can help maximize the efficiency of the natural immune system.

For example, people can strengthen the body's immune system through the use of supplements, such as natural herbs or vitamins. Some of the natural herbs that supposedly promote a healthier immune system include echinacea, from the cone flower plant, and astragalus, from a plant in the pea family. Vitamins, such as vitamins A, C and E, and some minerals, such as zinc, magnesium and selenium, have also been found to do this. Astragalus is rich in selenium, and this could be a reason for its effectiveness.

Another way in which the immune system may be strengthened is by improvements in lifestyle. Reducing intake of caffeine and alcohol, giving up smoking, exercising more and getting adequate sleep, sunshine and fresh air, can all have beneficial effects on the immune system.

A healthy digestive system contains millions of 'good' bacteria. These prevent harmful bacteria from entering the body. Without these good bacteria, we are much more likely to develop infections from harmful bacteria. Antibiotics kill good bacteria as well as

CUTTING EDGE   FACTS

Honey and wounds

Since the earliest times, people have tried to find ways of healing their injuries. Some of the old ideas seem strange to us now, and some have been found to have no real medical value. However, scientists have discovered that some really do work and have investigated the reasons for their effectiveness. For example, putting honey on wounds was once regarded as a standard remedy. People believed that the honey would help to clean and heal the wound. This may not sound a very clean and hygienic thing to do, but modern research has shown that there is a scientific basis for this: honey contains a chemical called hydrogen peroxide that prevents infection.

harmful ones and so, after a course of antibiotics, our natural gut bacteria may be depleted. They can be replenished by eating products such as 'live' yoghurts and drinks, or by eating the good bacteria that are found on the skins of many fruit and vegetables, such as apples and potatoes.

Herbal tea can be made from dried eucalyptus leaves, which have antiseptic properties.

CHAPTER 4

Producing Antibiotics, Vaccines and other Anti-infection Medicines

Antibiotics, vaccines and other anti-infection medicines are produced on a vast commercial scale. The whole process is carefully regulated and monitored at every stage to ensure that the medicines are safe for us to use. Advances in modern technology have improved production methods and have made significant contributions to the research into new medicines to combat infectious diseases.

Developing antibiotics

Since Alexander Fleming discovered the antibiotic properties of penicillin, many other scientists have been involved in the development of these medicines. Fleming himself was unable to

CUTTING EDGE   FACTS

Testing antibiotics

Until the development of modern computers, chemicals were tested in the laboratory to see if they showed antibiotic activity. The chemical was mixed into a culture gel (a substance on which bacteria can grow) and small samples of different bacteria were placed on it. If the chemical was to have any value as an antibiotic, it had to prevent the growth of at least one of the bacteria samples. This method was slow and laborious. Now, computer modelling techniques can be used to predict which chemicals are likely to have antibiotic properties. Computer-controlled robotic equipment can handle vast numbers of samples and test them more quickly and efficiently than human researchers could.

A researcher tests the sensitivity of bacteria to different antibiotics.

purify enough penicillin to allow him to test its use as a medicine. Two other scientists, Howard Florey and Ernst Chain, developed a method for doing this, but penicillin was not produced on a commercial scale until World War II.

Doctors often refer to 'families of antibiotics'. In other words, many antibiotics are closely related medications that share a common molecular core structure. US scientist Lloyd H. Conover first discovered this relationship in 1955 while studying antibiotics called terramycin and aureomycin. He named their core structure 'tetracycline'. Other scientists soon discovered a different core for penicillin, which they called beta-lactam. Researchers often develop new antibiotics by slightly modifying such core structures.

The discovery of these cores gave rise to a whole new range of antibiotics for use in the fight against infectious diseases. Some are extracted from fungi, some from other living things such as bacteria and plants, while others are synthesized in the laboratory.

Testing for safety

Before an antibiotic can be produced commercially, scientists have to be very sure that it is safe and will not have any harmful side effects (effects other than those intended) on patients. Side effects caused by drugs can range from minor problems, such as increased thirstiness, sweating and headache, to much more serious complications, such as anaemia, permanent liver damage and hearing loss, and in extreme cases, even death.

Initially, tests are carried out on cell cultures in the laboratory. The genetic material from the treated cells is tested to see whether

CUTTING EDGE   DEBATES

Are animal tests necessary?
When your doctor prescribes a medicine, you want to be sure that there is no risk it will harm you in any way. The safety of drugs can only be achieved by carrying out exhaustive tests. Although many tests can be carried out in cell cultures, these do not provide information about how a drug may affect a body system or complete organism. Without this information, many people argue that it would be too risky to move straight from cell tests to human tests. They say that this justifies the need for testing new drugs on animals. Other people argue that it is wrong to use animals in this way. The issue is still being debated.

What do you think?

they are damaged. If the antibiotic is found to have any adverse effects, it is abandoned and not tested any further. These initial cell culture tests also help the scientists to calculate the best dosages to use, so that people will not take too much or too little of the antibiotic.

If no adverse effects are detected, testing of the antibiotic on animals can proceed. Usually, small animals such as mice are used first. If the antibiotic causes no adverse effects, tests can proceed to larger animals, such as guinea pigs and rabbits.

Eventually, once an enormous number of cell tests and animal tests have been carried out, and the researchers are as confident as possible that the new antibiotic will be safe in humans, they test it on humans. Participants, or subjects, who are usually paid for the risk they will be taking, take part in a study called a clinical trial. To minimize the risk, these studies only involve a small number of people. If the subjects suffer no bad effects from the tests, studies involving larger numbers of people can be carried out.

With larger-scale clinical trials, subjects are usually divided into groups. Some subjects are given the new medicine while others are given a placebo (a drug containing no active ingredients). These trials are usually carried out on a 'double blind' basis. This means that subjects are given code numbers, and the patients, researchers and medical staff do not know to which group each subject is

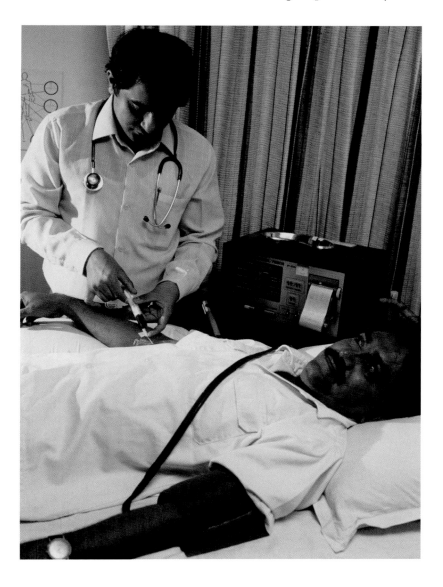

A blood sample is being taken from a patient who is taking part in a clinical trial.

assigned. Again, medicines and placebos are coded so that they cannot be identified. At the end of the trial, the information is decoded and scientists can see whether the new medicine was any more effective than the placebo.

Production of medicines

Once scientists are sure that the new medicine is both effective and safe, large-scale production can take place. The commercial production of antibiotics by fungi takes place in huge containers called fermentation tanks. These contain a liquid called growth medium, which provides all the nutrients the fungi need for growth.

For the maximum amount of antibiotic to be produced, the fungi must be kept in ideal conditions. To achieve this, factors such as the amount of oxygen present, temperature, acidity and nutrient levels are monitored and controlled very carefully. Eventually, the fungi come to the end of their life, and die. The antibiotic, which is a

When working with dangerous microbes, scientists use high-security cabinets like these to prevent infection and contamination.

chemical by-product of the fungi, is then extracted from the culture and purified.

Chemical synthesis of antibiotics also takes place on a vast scale. There are often several stages in the process of converting the extracted chemicals into the final antibiotic.

Vaccine production also takes place commercially on a vast scale. The first step is the isolation of the pathogen against which the vaccine is to offer protection. Once the pathogen has been isolated, it is grown in large vats called biofermentation tanks. As with antibiotic production from fungi, the conditions in the vats must be absolutely right to ensure that optimal growth occurs. Host cells, such as other micro-organisms, must be provided for the growth of viruses, as they cannot replicate outside a cell.

The pathogen cannot be used in its natural state because that would cause a full infection. Instead, the pathogen material must be attenuated – changed, weakened or killed. The attenuated virus is then mixed with other chemicals and the resulting material forms the basis of the vaccine.

Each batch of vaccine material is numbered and dated and then tested to ensure that it meets strict safety criteria. It is tested for effectiveness against the intended pathogens. Other testing ensures that it is at the correct strength, contains the right levels of all ingredients, and is not contaminated. Once the vaccine meets all these requirements, it is approved for clinical use.

CUTTING EDGE MOMENTS

Growing viruses in the laboratory

When viruses were first observed in the 1930s, it was difficult to study them because there was no easy way to obtain enough virus material. The problem arose because viruses only grow inside other cells. A breakthrough came in 1948 when a team of scientists working in America discovered that they could grow the mumps virus in fertilized chicken eggs. Virus material was injected into the eggs, and the virus multiplied inside the chick tissue. Using this method, it was possible to grow large quantities of the virus, allowing the study of viruses and the development of vaccines. Although better methods have since been developed, at the time this was a very important step in the science of virology.

Some vaccines offer protection against more than one disease. The MMR vaccine, for example, offers protection against measles, mumps and rubella. To achieve this, material from each of the pathogens the vaccine is to protect against must be mixed together. The finished vaccine is put into single-dose containers such as syringes or bottles.

Production of other anti-infection chemicals, such as antiseptics and antifungal medicines, is also carried out on a huge scale. As with antibiotic and vaccine production, much of the process is controlled by computer. Production lines, using similar technology to any other factory, produce very large quantities of the chemicals needed. These are then mixed with other substances to stabilize the

This doctor is prescribing a course of antibiotics to treat the patient's infection.

chemicals and to make the medicines suitable for use in whatever form they will be administered.

Testing and monitoring

Governments need to be sure that any medicines produced meet their own safety guidelines. Different governments have different sets of rules, but they all have the same aim: to protect the population by ensuring that all medicines produced are safe and will not cause harm to patients. Samples of antibiotic, vaccine material and all other new medicines are sent to government scientists or to other laboratories for testing. If the sample meets the required standards, packaging, marketing and distribution of the medicines can begin.

After their initial introduction in clinical trials, all medicines are monitored to make sure that no side effects appear at a later date. Doctors record information about any bad effects reported by their patients. If a pattern of side effects starts to become apparent, the medicine may be withdrawn for further testing or its use may be banned completely.

Medicines for treating infectious diseases are available in many different forms. They may be produced as tablets or capsules to take by mouth. Some are liquids given by injection, while others are creams that are rubbed onto the skin. Some are available in shampoos and other preparations. Doctors have up-to-date information about the medicines available for treating different conditions.

CUTTING EDGE　　　　FACTS

Overuse of antibiotics

Our reliance on antibiotics has contributed to the rise of antibiotic-resistant micro-organisms (see page 53). In an attempt to combat this problem, doctors are now advised only to prescribe antibiotics when absolutely necessary. Patients can help in this by not requesting antibiotics for minor infections and by completing a course of medication prescribed for an illness, even after they begin to feel better and the symptoms seem to have disappeared. Maintaining good personal hygiene can also help prevent infections occurring and spreading, and thus reduce the need for antibiotics.

CHAPTER 5

Overcoming Problems in Fighting Infectious Diseases

There are many problems that arise in the fight against infectious disease. Some are natural, and others are caused by humans. While scientists are working to reduce the incidence of infectious disease around the world and to develop new cures and treatments, other human activities are contributing to the spread of existing infectious diseases and to the creation of new ones.

Mutation

One major problem is micro-organism mutation. It affects both the use of antibiotics and the development of vaccines. If a bacterium mutates, or changes, into a new strain that is not affected by an antibiotic, then the antibiotic is of no further use in the treatment of that infection. This has occurred repeatedly over the years with a number of different bacteria and antibiotics. The problem was first reported during the 1950s, when bacteria mutated until penicillin no longer worked to kill them. These bactera had become 'resistant' to penicillin. Since then, more and more antibiotic-resistant bacterial strains have developed, making many of the older antibiotics useless. Probably the best-known antibiotic-resistant bacterial strain is MRSA (methicillin-

CUTTING EDGE   **SCIENCE**

What is mutation?

When a cell divides, its genetic material must be copied so that each new cell receives a full set of genetic information. If any errors occur during this copying process, the new cells will have different genetic information, and therefore slightly different characteristics, to the parent organism. These changes are called mutations. They can be caused by external factors such as exposure to radiation or chemicals. They can also arise naturally during the cell division process. Some mutations make it easier for a cell to survive, and so the numbers of the mutated cell type will increase.

resistant *Staphylococcus aureus*), which causes serious problems in many hospitals.

It is becoming increasingly difficult to find antibiotics that can be used to treat the resistant strains of bacteria. After the initial boom of antibiotic discoveries in the 1950s and 1960s, the rate of introduction of new antibiotics has slowed considerably. One reason for this is that the development and clinical trials of new antibiotics take many years and is very expensive. Consequently, pharmaceutical companies (manufacturers of medical drugs) are reducing their investment in this area.

Doctors are trying to overcome this problem by prescribing antibiotics only when absolutely necessary. Also, a much greater emphasis is now placed on maintaining high standards of cleanliness to reduce the spread of infectious diseases. This has generally been achieved by, among other things, regular hand-washing. However, recent research has shown that some bacteria, including MRSA, can survive in a waterborne micro-organism called amoeba. Any water, such as in flower vases and around sinks, could be harbouring amoeba, together with harmful bacteria. Because antiseptics do not kill amoeba, any bacteria inside the amoeba cells are effectively protected.

This micrograph shows MRSA cells undergoing cell division.

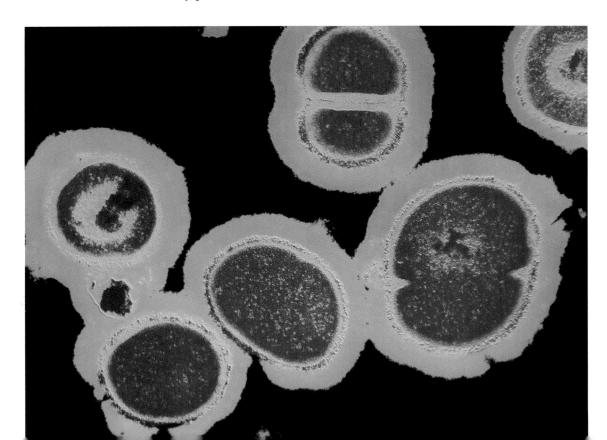

Viruses, such as influenza, also commonly mutate. Virus mutation makes vaccine development difficult. If a virus mutates into a new strain, the vaccine against the original may be ineffective against the new strain. Scientists then need to work quickly to develop a vaccine that is effective against the new strain. If this in turn mutates, another new vaccine will be needed. Vaccine researchers face a constant race to keep up with the mutations.

These WHO researchers in the Ivory Coast, Africa, are part of the Ebola virus research team. Collecting specimens like this Colobus monkey skull may help them to find the origin of the virus.

Traditional lifestyles and beliefs

Scientists and medical workers around the world work hard to implement vaccination and treatment programmes. They also try to raise people's awareness of the importance of hygiene and other health care issues. However, many cultures have their own deep-rooted beliefs and customs, and people are sometimes suspicious and distrustful of new ideas. This can slow down, prevent or even reverse an improvement in the health of a community. For example, in Nigeria the polio vaccination programme has been vigorously opposed by many local and religious groups. Where, until recently, the disease was being brought under control, its incidence is now increasing again because of such widespread misinformation. It has also spread from Nigeria to nearby areas where it had previously been eradicated (wiped out).

Human activity

Some human activities have actually made infectious diseases worse as well as causing the appearance and spread of new infectious diseases. As humans travel more widely and venture more deeply into wildlife habitats, they more frequently come into contact with infectious diseases in local animal populations. Some diseases, such as Rift Valley fever (which originated in Kenya, Africa), Marburg fever and Ebola virus (both of which originated in the Congo and Uganda in Africa), were originally animal diseases that have mutated in a way that has caused them to infect humans.

Wars and natural disasters such as famines and earthquakes often result in movements of large numbers of people from their homes to temporary accommodation centres. Lack of adequate water and sanitation at refugee camps can lead to outbreaks of infectious disease.

Global warming, and its associated climate changes, will also alter the patterns of infection. For example, if temperatures rise in many countries, then pathogens that were restricted to places with hot climates will be able to survive further afield.

CUTTING EDGE   SCIENTISTS

Donald Hopkins

Donald Hopkins was born in 1941 and wanted to be a doctor from as far back as he can remember. He studied at Morehouse College in Atlanta, Georgia, USA, and while a student, visited Egypt. Following his experiences on that trip, he decided to specialize in tropical diseases. Donald went on to study at the University of Chicago, Illinois, and at Harvard School of Public Health, Boston, Massachusetts. He began work in 1967 with the Smallpox Eradication Program in Sierra Leone, Africa. In 1969 he went back to Harvard as Assistant Professor of Tropical Public Health. Three years later he joined the US Centers for Disease Control (CDC), eventually becoming its Deputy Director. Donald has worked with several global health organizations and has been a major driving force in the campaign to combat parasitic Guinea worm infections worldwide. Thanks to the efforts of Donald Hopkins and his team, Guinea worm, which infected an estimated 3.5 million people in 1986, is now virtually eradicated, with only 11,500 cases reported in 2005.

CHAPTER 6

Current Developments

Around the world, many scientists are working to find new ways to prevent and treat infectious diseases. In laboratories, new chemicals are synthesized and tested. Computers are being used to predict useful chemical structures and to model patterns of disease spread and control. Ways of improving production methods are also being devised.

Micro-organisms are being studied in attempts to increase our understanding of them and thus our ability to combat them. The human immune system is being investigated in order to increase our understanding of how the body responds to infections. Geneticists – scientists who study the genetic material of humans and micro-organisms – hope this may give rise to new anti-infection techniques.

Scientists are also looking outside the laboratory for new ways to combat infectious disease. Some are studying traditional remedies used by native peoples, while others are investigating antibiotic chemicals found in animals (see pages 58–59).

New antibiotics

Chemists and computer specialists are working together to develop new antibiotic chemicals. Using existing antibiotic chemicals as a starting point, computers can help them predict the effects of making tiny changes to their structures. Chemists can then narrow their research to include only those chemicals pinpointed by the computers as being potentially useful, greatly improving efficiency.

Production improvements

Amazingly, space research has yielded information that may help in the production of antibiotics derived from fungi. From experiments carried out on the space shuttle, it was found that micro-organisms grow more quickly in zero-gravity conditions than on Earth. For example, the bacteria *Streptomyces plicatus* grows more quickly in space, producing the antibiotic actinomycin D at a faster rate than on Earth. Scientists are investigating why this happens, hoping that it will enable them to improve existing methods of producing antibiotics from fungi.

The immune system

The immune system relies on complex patterns of interactions between cells (see page 31). Research is being conducted to find out in more detail about the different cells involved and how they affect each other. Scientists hope to use this information to help them develop medicines that will boost the immune system and its response to infections.

Here, an astronaut is carrying out an experiment investigating fungal growth in almost zero-gravity conditions.

The Human Genome Project, completed in 2003, which mapped the full sequence of genes in humans, may help to further our understanding of the immune system. Scientists plan to study the genome to identify which genes are involved in the immune response and perhaps learn how to stimulate their action.

CUTTING EDGE   FACTS

Using mathematics and statistics

Mathematicians are using computer models to study the spread of infectious diseases and to predict the effects that different methods of controlling those diseases may have. This could be important if a pandemic infection breaks out, as it enables effective planning and monitoring of a worldwide response. A century and a half after the pioneering work of John Snow, the science of epidemiology is still proving invaluable in controlling infectious diseases.

Plasmids

Many bacteria contain tiny rings of genetic material called plasmids, which are separate from the genetic material that makes up the bacterial chromosome. Geneticists have found that some plasmids seem to be involved in the development of antibiotic resistance. A bacterial cell can contain one or many plasmids, which can be transferred from one bacterial cell to another, making each cell they enter resistant. Other plasmids can 'turn off' the resistance, making the bacteria sensitive to antibiotics again. Scientists think that it may be possible to use plasmids to overcome antibiotic resistance.

Studying traditional remedies

The world's rainforests contain a vast number of species of plants and animals, many of which are still unknown to scientists. Some have been used as traditional remedies by native peoples. One example of this is a plant called snakeroot, long used as a traditional medicine by the Seneca Nation of Native Americans, which has been found to have antibiotic and antifungal properties. Researchers often visit these places to gather information from native peoples and to collect plant samples. Back in the laboratory, the plant samples are analysed and the chemicals they contain are tested. It is possible that new medicines such as antibiotics may be discovered from this research.

CUTTING EDGE SCIENCE

Deadly saliva

The Komodo dragon, which is found in Indonesia, is the largest species of lizard in the world. The lizards are carnivores and often kill their prey in a single attack. They can kill just by biting because their saliva is deadly – it contains many different types of bacteria that infect and kill the prey. Scientists wondered why, if the saliva contains so many lethal bacteria, it does not harm the Komodo dragon itself. Samples of Komodo dragon saliva and blood are being analysed to find out whether they contain antibiotics or other chemicals that may protect the dragons. Scientists hope that this may lead to the discovery of new antibiotics that can be used to treat humans. Geneticists are also studying the dragon's genome to see whether it is genetically resistant to bacteria; if so, it may help in the development of a genetic therapy for infectious disease in humans.

The skin of this Amazonian tree frog produces chemicals that have antibiotic properties.

Learning from plants and animals

Another area of research focuses on the defence mechanisms used by different species of animal. Scientists hope that this will lead to the development of new modes of treatment and protection. For example, scientists studying capuchin monkeys from South America discovered that the monkeys rub millipedes into their skin at the time of year when insect bites are most common. When the chemicals in the millipedes were analysed, an insect-repellent chemical was found.

Scientists also study plant and animal species that appear to have a natural resistance to infection. They have found that many of them have antibiotic chemicals in their bodies. The first of these was discovered in 1986 in the skin of the African clawed frog of southern Africa, and was named magainin. Magainin is active against a wide range of pathogens including bacteria, protozoa and fungi. Since then, more antibiotic chemicals have been found in, for example, crocodile blood, seaweeds, pigs' guts and silk moths. These may be valuable in the development of future generations of antibiotics.

Glossary

antibiotic A chemical used to control bacterial infection.

antibody A chemical produced by white blood cells in response to an antigen.

antiseptic A chemical that kills micro-organisms.

antiviral Capable of destroying viruses, or making them inactive.

attenuate Produce a change in the natural potency of a virus that makes it incapable of causing disease.

bacteria A type of micro-organism that has a cell wall, a nucleus, its own DNA, and is capable of reproducing itself.

booster shot A repeat dose of a vaccine to maintain a person's level of immunity.

by-product Something produced as a secondary result of the production of something else.

carnivores Animals that eat other animals.

cell The smallest unit of a living thing.

colony A group of bacteria.

contraceptive Something used or taken to prevent a pregnancy.

culture The growing of biological material in the laboratory.

cytoplasm The parts of a plant or animal cell outside the nucleus.

endemic Occurring naturally in a particular place.

enzyme A chemical that carries out a chemical reaction in a living organism.

epidemic An outbreak of infectious disease affecting many people.

epidemiology The study of the spread and causes of diseases.

eradicated Destroyed or wiped out so that it can never recur.

famine A severe shortage of food resulting in widespread hunger.

ferment Use mico-organisms, such as yeasts, to break down a substance into simpler ones.

fission Splitting into two.

flagellae Slender, threadlike structures of many micro-organisms, used as a means of moving around.

fruiting bodies A part of certain fungi from which spores are released.

fungi A type of micro-organism that has hyphae instead of normal cells.

genetic Having to do with the passing of information from one generation to the next.

host cell A cell occupied by a virus or its genetic material in order for the virus to reproduce.

Human Genome Project Research carried out to map the complete set of human genes.

hygienic Relating to keeping clean.

hypodermic Relating to the area of tissue lying beneath the skin.

immune system The body's defence mechanisms.

incidence The frequency with which something occurs.

infectious Can spread from person to person.

intravenous Into a vein.

isolated Happening only rarely and unlikely to recur or prove a continuing problem.

larva A stage in the life cycle of some organisms.

lethal Causing or able to cause death.

localized infection An infection that affects only a small part of the body.

lymphocyte A type of white blood cell.

micro-organism A living organism that is too small to be seen with the naked eye.

microscope An instrument that magnifies tiny things.

nucleus The part of a cell that contains the genetic information.

nutrients Substances that provide nourishment, such as the ingredients of food that keep a body healthy and help it to grow.

oral Relating to the mouth.

organ A tissue or tissues that perform a single specific bodily function or related functions.

pandemic A widespread outbreak of a disease affecting a large number of people.

parasite An organism that lives off other organisms.

pathogen An organism that causes disease.

placebo An inactive chemical used in clinical trials.

plasmid A small circle of DNA, especially found in the cells of bacteria.

proteins An important group of substances that make up living structures such as skin, hair and muscle and also control processes inside cells.

protozoa A single-celled organism.

quarantine Keep away from others in order to prevent the spread of infection.

resistant Not affected by something, for example, a disease.

respiration (as in cellular respiration) The process by which a cell breaks down gl3ucose (a type of sugar) in order to obtain energy.

sanitation Methods for removing waste.

septic Full of or generating pus (fluid that forms at the site of an infection consisting of dead white blood cells, dead tissue and other substances).

side effects Usually undesirable secondary effecs of a drug or other form of medical treatment.

spores Small, usually one-celled reproductive structures produced by fungi, capable of developing into a new individual.

synthetic Not occurring naturally; human-made.

system Organs and tissues that work together to carry out a single function or related functions.

tissue Cells of one type organized to carry out a single function.

toxin A chemical produced by some micro-organisms that causes illness.

vaccine A substance used to produce immunity to a disease.

vector An organism, such as a mosquito, that transmits disease-causing micro-organisms from infected individuals to people, or from infected animals to human beings.

virus A type of micro-organism that can only reproduce inside a host cell.

Further Information

BOOKS

Amazing World of Microlife: Microlife that Makes Us Ill by Steve Parker (Raintree, 2006)

Body Talk: Defend Yourself by Steve Parker (Raintree, 2006)

Microlife: Fighting Infectious Disease by Robert Snedden (Heinemann Library, 2000)

Micro-world: Microscopic Life in Your Body by Brian Ward (Franklin Watts, 2003)

Science at the Edge: Fight Against Disease by Sally Morgan (Heinemann Library, 2003)

21st Century Debates: World Health by Ronan Foley (Hodder Wayland, 2002)

WEBSITES

www.kidshealth.org
This website provides information about many aspects of health that may affect young people.

www.microbe.org
This website provides a wealth of information and activities about micro-organisms and the scientists who study them.

www.microbeworld.org
This website takes you on a journey into the world of micro-organisms.

www.pfizerfunzone.com
This website covers a range of science topics, together with activities and experiments. You need Shockwave to access this site.

Index

Index *(continued)*